Entertainment Industry Facts

Entertainment Industry Facts

Joann Williams

Joann Williams
Entertainment Industry Facts

Published by Spines
ISBN 979-8-89569-648-4

Contents

Disclaimer

This book is intended to provide a General overview of the music industry and offer Basic Guidance.

For those interested in starting a career in Music. It does not constitute professional legal or financial advice. The music industry is constantly evolving, and individual experiences may vary. Readers are encouraged to consult with experts in specific areas, such as Entertainment Attorneys, Accounts, and music industry professionals, for personalized advice in 2024.

Disclaimer

About the Author

Joann Williams is a Seasoned music and Entertainment industry professional with over 20 years of experience. As a New Jersey native, she has cultivated her career within the dynamic landscape of the Music Industry.

Currently based in Georgia, Joann Williams has made contributions to the world of music and entertainment, showcasing her talent.

Joann Williams had the opportunity to host:

Hosting R&B Showcases.
Casting Calls.
Management.
Artist Development.
Director of Artist & Repertoire.
And much more…

Entertainment Industry Facts

OPEN

TO GET RIGHT INTO MUSIC BUSINESS

RESEARCH – READ - STUDY – REPEAT

Entertainment Get Right Contents

THIS BOOK WILL GUIDE you in starting your music career and what you need to do first.

1. Register Your (Stage Name) LLC
2. Get your EIN number
3. Copyright your music

•

1. For L.L.C.: Go to your County Clerk and tell them you want to register your business name (which is your stage name). You will also need to get it notarized. Do it all on the same day. You need your ID (at least 2): Driver's license, Passport, and Birth Certificate.
2. Suppose you have a Budget Trademark and your stage name. Go to the Library of Congress and file with them. If you have any questions, they can assist you.

Entertainment Get Right with Business

1. Register Your Stage Name
2. File Your Employee identification number
3. Copyright your Music as an album, and then pick songs from your album as a Single. 7 – 29 songs are on an Album.
4. Also, have two (2) copies of your Personal Documents.
5. Diver License
6. Birth Certificate
7. If you don't have a passport

APPLY for your passport. 6 weeks or more depends. Ask for a rush if you have to Perform outside the United States. Have your paperwork, and also have a printout where you will be performing your printout from your airlines that shows you need a rush for your passport.

Look up page

HERE IS A LIST. Look into it.

Research – Read – Study

1. Copyright: Learn it and understand what you are reading.

If you are not sure, ask.

2. If you have a Logo, Register your Brand.

Always ask Questions.

3. The split sheet, which goes by many Names, is when you work with a group or individual. And you add words or a verse. Form an agreement between the individual or group. When signed, it's legally binding. (Read up on This)

Be prepared to have your split sheet.

AGREEMENT IDENTIFIES Contributors

When you are in the studio, are there any other locations where you do any of the following: Versa, any bars, Melodies, or song ownership? When you do this, it becomes legally binding. Do your research!

Business Information

COPYRIGHT

Trademark

Passport

Intellectual Property

Infringement

Employee Identification Number

(EIN)

Management

STAGE NAME

Bank Account

Credit

Lawyer

Publishing

Public Relations

Writers Group

Trademark

TRADEMARK: understand the difference between a copyright/trademark.

TRADEMARK

Select the Name you want to trademark. Conduct a Name search.

Identify the goods and services and filing basic. Do your research. If you have the budget, get a lawyer to apply for you.

Intellectual Property

1. Patent
2. Trademark
3. Copyright
4. Trade Secrets

WHO OWNS INTELLECTUAL PROPERTY?
The Creator, Developer or Investor.

ALWAYS GET PERMISSION FROM THE OWNER.

LEGAL FORMS FROM A (LAWYER).

Intellectual Property Rights

1. Copyrights
2. Trademark
3. Patents
4. Plant Varieties
5. Industrial
6. Designs
7. Semiconductors

Violations of Intellectual Property

COPYRIGHTS/ Infringement/ Trademark Infringement/ And Patent Infringement

WHO OWNS INTELLECTUAL PROPERTY

The creator, Developer, or Inventory.

ALWAYS GET PERMISSION FROM THE OWNER IN LEGAL forms.

Electronic Press Kit

IT'S About you and your Music.

Have 1 – 2 Songs (Best Songs)

YOUR PERSONAL MUSIC INFORMATION

Phone Number

Email

Social media Platforms

THE ELECTRONIC PRESS KIT GOES ON YOUR CELL PHONE.

It must be easy to Exchange your information.

Businesses

1. You need a team that's loyal to you 100%.
2. Social media all platforms
3. You will need two people, one for your emails and one for your social media team.
4. Hype Man
5. Make sure you keep your paperwork with you at all times.

RESEARCH – Read – Study

MAKING IT YOUR OWN WILL GIVE YOU CONFIDENCE. BUT always do it right!

Business language

MAKE sure you have (2) bank accounts.

1. Personal Bank Account
2. Business Bank Account

THE BUSINESS ACCOUNT IS FOR EVERYTHING YOU DO IN your Music Career.

KEEP THEM SEPARATE. IT'S FOR TAX PURPOSES.

Learn Music Business Language

ONCE YOUR MUSIC Career has a position, into getting signed by a label, get yourself an Entertainment lawyer and not from within any label. Get you a Public Relations from a well-known firm.

OPTIONAL

Gym
Choreography Instructor
Acting Classes
Doing all of this can enhance your career.

Understand What you have learned.

NAME The three most important things to do first.

1)

2)

3)

Do a Budget for Yourself:

Social Media, Stay on top of your Accounts:

1.
2.
3.
4.
5.
6.
7.
8.
9.
10.

Record Labels List Top 10:

1.
2.
3.
4.
5.
6.
7.
8.
9.
10.

Radio Stations, Get a List:

1.
2.
3.
4.
5.
6.
7.
8.
9.
10.

Keep a List of Dee Jay's:

1.
2.
3.
4.
5.
6.
7.
8.
9.
10.

Check your Credit Every 3 Months

KEEP a record and update

Check your Credit Every 3 Months

KEEP a record and update

Keep a List (Which is your Music catalog)

Singles

Extended Play (EP)

What most will call 4-6 songs (Tracks)

Albums 7 – 29 or more

Important Phone Numbers:

1.
2.
3.
4.
5.
6.
7.
8.
9.
10.

Appointment Log Sheet

NAMES ADDRESS PHONE * Date:

1.
2.
3.
4.
5.
6.
7.
8.
9.
10.

Appointment Log Sheet

NAMES ADDRESS PHONE * Date:

1.
2.
3.
4.
5.
6.
7.
8.
9.
10.

Learn About Your Music Business

TAKE NOTES:

Take Notes Sheet

Reminder For Yourself

Your Dream is Your Dream
Get all the information that can
Enhance your future.

This facts Sheets will Guide you
Too many levels you need in this
Entertainment industry.

REMINDER TO YOURSELF.

Read, Study, Learn.
Add. Apply.

If you are not sure, Get a Lawyer.

Let's begin

Remember The Facts

Entertainment Industry Facts

THERE WILL BE a follow up Book (2)

Things you need to Look up.

- Get your Social media numbers up.
- Look into distribution to market your music.
- Look up license Music Services.
- Then, pick what you like.
- Research, Read, Study.
- Copyright the lyrics, Music, and Cover Art.
- Press release to the media.
- Promote the Music on Digital.
- Stream your Music.
- Only Post your Music when:

COPYRIGHT

RESEARCH. READ. STUDY.

ttover2000@gmail.com

I want to dedicate this book to
Jahsiah, Journey, Winona, Joel and Aniyah.

www.ingramcontent.com/pod-product-compliance
Lightning Source LLC
LaVergne TN
LVHW010509160826
845677LV00012B/2743
* 9 7 9 8 8 9 5 6 9 6 4 8 4 *